D1779157

MODERN
FILM
SCRIPTS

THE SEVENTH SEAL
a film by
Ingmar Bergman

translated from the Swedish
by Lars Malmström and David Kushner

Simon and Schuster, New York

All rights reserved including the right
of reproduction in whole or in part in any form
English translation copyright © 1960 by Ingmar Bergman
Original Swedish language film entitled *Det Sjunde Inseglet*
© 1956 by Ingmar Bergman
Published by Simon and Schuster
Rockefeller Center, 630 Fifth Avenue,
New York, New York 10020
Fifth Printing

Library of Congress Catalog Card Number: 68-9176

This edition is for sale only in the United States of America,
its territories, possessions, protectorates and places mandated to it,
the Philippines and the Dominion of Canada

Manufactured in Great Britain by Villiers Publications Ltd,
London NW5

The publishers wish to express their gratitude for the help and co-operation received from the staff of Janus Films, Inc., particularly Cyrus Harvey Jr., and also Peter Cowie and the British Film Institute

NOTE: The screenplay in this book is identical to that used by Ingmar Bergman when filming, except that: (1) the original script contains numbers before each sequence which indicate the estimated number of shots that will be necessary for that sequence; (2) since this screenplay is prepared before shooting begins, it contains sequences and dialogue which do not appear in the final film; Bergman has deleted some material to make the published script conform to the film.

CONTENTS

Introduction: Ingmar Bergman 8
Credits 10
Cast 11
The Seventh Seal 13

INTRODUCTION

People ask what are my intentions with my films — my aims. It is a difficult and dangerous question, and I usually give an evasive answer: I try to tell the truth about the human condition, the truth as I see it. This answer seems to satisfy everyone, but it is not quite correct. I prefer to describe what I *would like* my aim to be.

There is an old story of how the cathedral of Chartres was struck by lightning and burned to the ground. Then thousands of people came from all points of the compass, like a giant procession of ants, and together they began to rebuild the cathedral on its old site. They worked until the building was completed—master builders, artists, labourers, clowns, noblemen, priests, burghers. But they all remained anonymous, and no one knows to this day who built the cathedral of Chartres.

Regardless of my own beliefs and my own doubts, which are unimportant in this connection, it is my opinion that art lost its basic creative drive the moment it was separated from worship. It severed an umbilical cord and now lives its own sterile life, generating and degenerating itself. In former days the artist remained unknown and his work was to the glory of God. He lived and died without being more or less important than other artisans; 'eternal values,' 'immortality' and 'masterpiece' were terms not applicable in his case. The ability to create was a gift. In such a world flourished invulnerable assurance and natural humility.

Today the individual has become the highest form and the greatest bane of artistic creation. The smallest wound or pain of the ego is examined under a microscope as if it were of eternal importance. The artist considers his isolation, his subjectivity, his individualism almost holy. Thus we finally gather in one large pen, where we stand and bleat about our loneliness without listening to each other and without realising that we are smothering each other to death. The individualists stare into each other's eyes and yet deny the existence of each other. We walk in circles, so limited by our own anxieties that we can no longer distinguish between true and false, between the gangster's whim and the purest ideal.

Thus if I am asked what I would like the general purpose of my films to be, I would reply that I want to be one of the artists in the cathedral on the great plain. I want to make a dragon's head, an angel, a devil — or perhaps a saint — out of stone. It does not matter which; it is the sense of satisfaction that counts. Regardless of whether I believe or not, whether I am a Christian or not, I would play my part in the collective building of the cathedral.

INGMAR BERGMAN

CREDITS:

Screenplay	Ingmar Bergman
Director	Ingmar Bergman
Assistant director	Lennart Ohlsson
Director of Photography	Gunnar Fischer
Assistant cameraman	Åke Nilsson
Music	Erik Nordgren
Music directed by	Sixten Ehrling
Choreography	Else Fisher
Sets	P. A. Lundgren
Costumes	Manne Lindholm
Make-up	Nils Nittel and Carl M. Lundh, Inc.
Sound	Aaby Wedin and Lennart Wallin
Special sound effects	Evald Andersson
Editor	Lennart Wallén
Produced by	Svensk Filmindustri
Distributed by	Janus Films Inc., in the United States, and by Gala Films Ltd., in Great Britain
Running time	96 minutes

CAST:

Jöns, the squire	Gunnar Björnstrand
Death	Bengt Ekerot
Jof	Nils Poppe
The knight, Antonius Block	Max von Sydow
Mia	Bibi Andersson
Lisa	Inga Gill
Tyan, the witch	Maud Hansson
The knight's wife	Inga Landgré
The girl	Gunnel Lindblom
Raval	Bertil Anderberg
The monk	Anders Ek
Plog, the smith	Åke Fridell
The church painter	Gunnar Olsson
Skat	Erik Strandmark
The merchant	Benkt-Åke Benktsson
Woman at the inn	Gudrun Brost
Leader of the soldiers	Ulf Johansson
The young monk	Lars Lind

THE SEVENTH SEAL

The night had brought little relief from the heat, and at dawn a hot gust of wind blows across the colourless sea. The KNIGHT, Antonius Block, lies prostrate on some spruce branches spread over the fine sand. His eyes are wide-open and bloodshot from lack of sleep.
Nearby his squire JONS is snoring loudly. He has fallen asleep where he collapsed, at the edge of the forest among the wind-gnarled fir trees. His open mouth gapes towards the dawn, and unearthly sounds come from his throat.
At the sudden gust of wind the horses stir, stretching their parched muzzles towards the sea. They are as thin and worn as their masters.
The KNIGHT has risen and waded into the shallow water, where he rinses his sunburned face and blistered lips.
JONS rolls over to face the forest and the darkness. He moans in his sleep and vigorously scratches the stubbled hair on his head. A scar stretches diagonally across his scalp, as white as lightning against the grime.
The KNIGHT returns to the beach and falls on his knees. With his eyes closed and brow furrowed, he says his morning prayers. His hands are clenched together and his lips form the words silently. His face is sad and bitter. He opens his eyes and stares directly into the morning sun which wallows up from the misty sea like some bloated, dying fish. The sky is grey and immobile, a dome of lead. A cloud hangs mute and dark over the western horizon. High up, barely visible, a seagull floats on motionless wings. Its cry is weird and restless.
The KNIGHT'S large grey horse lifts its head and whinnies. Antonius Block turns around.
Behind him stands a man in black. His face is very pale

and he keeps his hands hidden in the wide folds of his cloak.
KNIGHT: Who are you?
DEATH: I am Death.
KNIGHT: Have you come for me?
DEATH: I have been walking by your side for a long time.
KNIGHT: That I know.
DEATH: Are you prepared?
KNIGHT: My body is frightened, but I am not.
DEATH: Well, there is no shame in that.
The KNIGHT has risen to his feet. He shivers. DEATH opens his cloak to place it around the KNIGHT's shoulders.
KNIGHT: Wait a moment.
DEATH: That's what they all say. I grant no reprieves.
KNIGHT: You play chess, don't you?
A gleam of interest kindles in DEATH's eyes.
DEATH: How did you know that?
KNIGHT: I have seen it in paintings and heard it sung in ballads.
DEATH: Yes, in fact I'm quite a good chess player.
KNIGHT: But you can't be better than I am.
The KNIGHT rummages in the big black bag which he keeps beside him and takes out a small chessboard. He places it carefully on the ground and begins setting up the pieces.
DEATH: Why do you want to play chess with me?
KNIGHT: I have my reasons.
DEATH: That is your privilege.
KNIGHT: The condition is that I may live as long as I hold out against you. If I win, you will release me. Is it agreed?
The KNIGHT holds out his two fists to DEATH, who smiles at him suddenly. DEATH points to one of the KNIGHT's hands; it contains a black pawn.
KNIGHT: You drew black!
DEATH: Very appropriate. Don't you think so?
The KNIGHT and DEATH bend over the chessboard. After a moment of hesitation, Antonius Block opens with his

king's pawn. DEATH *moves, also using his king's pawn.*

The morning breeze has died down. The restless movement of the sea has ceased, the water is silent. The sun rises from the haze and its glow whitens. The sea gull floats under the dark cloud, frozen in space. The day is already scorchingly hot.
The squire JONS *is awakened by a kick in the rear. Opening his eyes, he grunts like a pig and yawns broadly. He scrambles to his feet, saddles his horse and picks up the heavy pack.*
The KNIGHT *slowly rides away from the sea, into the forest near the beach and up towards the road. He pretends not to hear the morning prayers of his squire.* JONS *soon overtakes him.*

JONS *sings*: Between a strumpet's legs to lie
            Is the life for which I sigh.
He stops and looks at his master, but the KNIGHT *hasn't heard* JON'S *song, or he pretends that he hasn't. To give further vent to his irritation,* JONS *sings even louder.*

JONS *sings*: Up above is God Almighty
            So very far away,
            But your brother the Devil
            You will meet on every level.
JONS *finally gets the* KNIGHT'S *attention. He stops singing. The* KNIGHT, *his horse,* JONS'S *own horse and* JONS *himself know all the songs by heart. The long, dusty journey from the Holy Land hasn't made them any cleaner.*
They ride across a mossy heath which stretches towards the horizon. Beyond it, the sea lies shimmering in the white glitter of the sun.
JONS: In Färjestad everyone was talking about evil omens and other horrible things. Two horses had eaten each other in the night, and, in the churchyard, graves had been opened and the remains of corpses scattered all over the place. Yesterday afternoon there were as many as four suns in the heavens.

The KNIGHT *doesn't answer. Close by, a scrawny dog is whining, crawling towards its master, who is sleeping in a sitting position in the blazing hot sun. A black cloud of flies clusters around his head and shoulders. The miserable-looking dog whines incessantly as it lies flat on its stomach, wagging its tail.*

JONS *dismounts and approaches the sleeping man.* JONS *addresses him politely. When he doesn't receive an answer, he walks up to the man in order to shake him awake. He bends over the sleeping man's shoulder, but quickly pulls back his hand. The man falls backward on the heath, his face turned towards* JONS. *It is a corpse, staring at* JONS *with empty eye sockets and white teeth.*

JONS *remounts and overtakes his master. He takes a drink from his waterskin and hands the bag to the knight.*

KNIGHT: Well, did he show you the way?
JONS: Not exactly.
KNIGHT: What did he say?
JONS: Nothing.
KNIGHT: Was he a mute?
JONS: No, sir, I wouldn't say that. As a matter of fact, he was quite eloquent.
KNIGHT: Oh?
JONS: He was eloquent, all right. The trouble is that what he had to say was most depressing.
JONS *sings:* One moment you're bright and lively,
The next you're crawling with worms.
Fate is a terrible villain
And you, my friend, its poor victim.
KNIGHT: Must you sing?
JONS: No.

The KNIGHT *hands his squire a piece of bread, which keeps him quiet for a while. The sun burns down on them cruelly, and beads of perspiration trickle down their faces. There is a cloud of dust around the horses' hooves.*

They ride past an inlet and along verdant groves. In the

shade of some large trees stands a bulging wagon covered with a mottled canvas. A horse whinnies nearby and is answered by the KNIGHT'S *horse. The two travellers do not stop to rest under the shade of the trees but continue riding until they disappear at the bend of the road.*

In his sleep, JOF *the juggler hears the neighing of his horse and the answer from a distance. He tries to go on sleeping, but it is stifling inside the wagon. The rays of the sun filtering through the canvas cast streaks of light across the face of* JOF'S *wife,* MIA, *and their one-year-old son,* MIKAEL, *who are sleeping deeply and peacefully. Near them,* JONAS SKAT, *an older man, snores loudly.*

JOF *crawls out of the wagon. There is still a spot of shade under the big trees. He takes a drink of water, gargles, stretches and talks to his scrawny old horse.*

JOF: Good morning. Have you had breakfast? I can't eat grass, worse luck. Can't you teach me how? We're a little hard up. People aren't very interested in juggling in this part of the country.

He has picked up the juggling balls and slowly begins to toss them. Then he stands on his head and cackles like a hen. Suddenly he stops and sits down with a look of utter astonishment on his face. The wind causes the trees to sway slightly. The leaves stir and there is a soft murmur. The flowers and the grass bend gracefully, and somewhere a bird raises its voice in a long warble.

JOF'S *face breaks into a smile and his eyes fill with tears. With a dazed expression he sits flat on his behind while the grass rustles softly, and bees and butterflies hum around his head. The unseen bird continues to sing.*

Suddenly the breeze stops blowing, the bird stops singing, JOF'S *smile fades, the flowers and grass wilt in the heat. The old horse is still walking around grazing and swishing its tail to ward off the flies.*

JOF *comes to life. He rushes into the wagon and shakes*

MIA *awake*.

JOF: Mia, wake up. Wake up! Mia, I've just seen something. I've got to tell you about it!

MIA *sits up, terrified*: What is it? What's happened?

JOF: Listen, I've had a vision. No, it wasn't a vision. It was real, absolutely real.

MIA: Oh, so you've had a vision again!

> MIA'S *voice is filled with gentle irony.* JOF *shakes his head and grabs her by the shoulders.*

JOF: But I did see her!

MIA: Whom did you see?

JOF: The Virgin Mary.

> MIA *can't help being impressed by her husband's fervour. She lowers her voice.*

MIA: Did you really see her?

JOF: She was so close to me that I could have touched her. She had a golden crown on her head and wore a blue gown with flowers of gold. She was barefoot and had small brown hands with which she was holding the Child and teaching Him to walk. And then she saw me watching her and she smiled at me. My eyes filled with tears and when I wiped them away, she had disappeared. And everything became so still in the sky and on the earth. Can you understand . . .

MIA: What an imagination you have.

JOF: You don't believe me! But it was real, I tell you, not the kind of reality you see every day, but a different kind.

MIA: Perhaps it was the kind of reality you told us about when you saw the Devil painting our wagon wheels red, using his tail as a brush.

JOF *embarrassed*: Why must you keep bringing that up?

MIA: And then you discovered that you had red paint under your nails.

JOF: Well, perhaps that time I made it up. *Eagerly*. I did it just so that you would believe in my other visions. The real ones. The ones that I didn't make up.

MIA *severely*: You have to keep your visions under control.

Otherwise people will think that you're a half-wit, which you're not. At least not yet — as far as I know. But, come to think of it, I'm not so sure about that.

JOF *angry*: I didn't ask to have visions. I can't help it if voices speak to me, if the Holy Virgin appears before me and angels and devils like my company.

SKAT *sits up*: Haven't I told you once and for all that I need my morning's sleep! I have asked you politely, pleaded with you, but nothing works. So now I'm telling you to *shut up!*

> *His eyes are popping with rage. He turns over and continues snoring where he left off.* MIA *and* JOF *decide that it would be wisest to leave the wagon. They sit down on a crate.* MIA *has* MIKAEL *on her knees. He is naked and squirms vigorously.* JOF *sits close to his wife. Slumped over, he still looks dazed and astonished. A dry, hot wind blows from the sea.*

MIA: If we would only get some rain. Everything is burned to cinders. We won't have anything to eat this winter.

JOF *yawning*: We'll get by.

> *He says this smilingly, with a casual air. He stretches and laughs contentedly.*

MIA: I want Mikael to have a better life than ours.

JOF: Mikael will grow up to be a great acrobat — or a juggler who can do the one impossible trick.

MIA: What's that?

JOF: To make one of the balls stand absolutely still in the air.

MIA: But that's impossible.

JOF: Impossible for us — but not for him.

MIA: You're dreaming again.

> *She yawns. The sun has made her a bit drowsy and she lies down on the grass.* JOF *does likewise and puts one arm around his wife's shoulders.*

JOF: I've composed a song. I made it up during the night when I couldn't sleep. Do you want to hear it?

MIA: Sing it. I'm very curious.

JOF: I have to sit up first.
He sits with his legs crossed, makes a dramatic gesture with his arms and sings in a loud voice.
JOF: On a lily branch a dove is perched
   Against the summer sky,
   She sings a wondrous song of Christ
   And there's great joy on high.
He interrupts his singing in order to be complimented by his wife.
JOF: Mia! Are you asleep?
MIA: It's a lovely song.
JOF: I haven't finished yet.
MIA: I heard it, but I think I'll sleep a little longer. You can sing the rest to me afterwards.
JOF: All you do is sleep.
JOF is a bit offended and glances over at his son, MIKAEL, but he is also sleeping soundly in the high grass. JONAS SKAT comes out from the wagon. He yawns; he is very tired and in a bad humour. In his hands he holds a crudely made death mask.
SKAT: Is this supposed to be a mask for an actor? If the priests didn't pay us so well, I'd say no thank you.
JOF: Are you going to play Death?
SKAT: Just think, scaring decent folk out of their wits with this kind of nonsense.
JOF: When are we supposed to do this play?
SKAT: At the saints' feast in Elsinore. We're going to perform right on the church steps, believe it or not.
JOF: Wouldn't it be better to play something bawdy? People like it better, and, besides, it's more fun.
SKAT: Idiot. There's a rumour going around that there's a terrible pestilence in the land, and now the priests are prophesying sudden death and all sorts of spiritual agonies.
MIA is awake now and lies contentedly on her back, sucking on a blade of grass and looking smilingly at her husband.

JOF: And what part am I to play?
SKAT: You're such a damn fool, so you're going to be the Soul of Man.
JOF: That's a bad part, of course.
SKAT: Who makes the decisions around here? Who is the director of this company anyhow?
>   SKAT, *grinning, holds the mask in front of his face and recites dramatically.*

SKAT: Bear this in mind, you fool. Your life hangs by a thread. Your time is short. *In his usual voice.* Are the women going to like me in this getup. Will I make a hit? No! I feel as if I were dead already.
>   *He stumbles into the wagon muttering furiously.* JOF *sits, leaning forward.* MIA *lies beside him on the grass.*

MIA: Jof!
JOF: What is it?
MIA: Sit still. Don't move.
JOF: What do you mean?
MIA: Don't say anything.
JOF: I'm as silent as a grave.
MIA: Shh! I love you.

>   *Waves of heat envelop the grey stone church in a strange white mist. The* KNIGHT *dismounts and enters. After tying up the horses,* JONS *slowly follows him in. When he comes onto the church porch he stops in surprise. To the right of the entrance there is a large fresco on the wall, not quite finished. Perched on a crude scaffolding is a* PAINTER *wearing a red cap and paint-stained clothes. He has one brush in his mouth, while with another in his hand he outlines a small, terrified human face amidst a sea of other faces.*

JONS: What is this supposed to represent?
PAINTER: The Dance of Death.
JONS: And that one is Death?
PAINTER: Yes, he dances off with all of them.

Jons: Why do you paint such nonsense?
Painter: I thought it would serve to remind people that they must die.
Jons: Well, it's not going to make them feel any happier.
Painter: Why should one always make people happy? It might not be a bad idea to scare them a little once in a while.
Jons: Then they'll close their eyes and refuse to look at your painting.
Painter: Oh, they'll look. A skull is almost more interesting than a naked woman.
Jons: If you do scare them...
Painter: They'll think.
Jons: And if they think...
Painter: They'll become still more scared.
Jons: And then they'll run right into the arms of the priests.
Painter: That's not my business.
Jons: You're only painting your Dance of Death.
Painter: I'm only painting things as they are. Everyone else can do as he likes.
Jons: Just think how some people will curse you.
Painter: Maybe. But then I'll paint something amusing for them to look at. I have to make a living — at least until the plague takes me.
Jons: The plague. That sounds horrible.
Painter: You should see the boils on a diseased man's throat. You should see how his body shrivels up so that his legs look like knotted strings — like the man I've painted over there.

The Painter points with his brush. Jons sees a small human form writhing in the grass, its eyes turned upwards in a frenzied look of horror and pain.

Jons: That looks terrible.
Painter: It certainly does. He tries to rip out the boil, he bites his hands, tears his veins open with his fingernails and his screams can be heard everywhere. Does that scare you?

Jons: Scare? Me? You don't know me. What are the horrors you've painted over there?

Painter: The remarkable thing is that the poor creatures think the pestilence is the Lord's punishment. Mobs of people who call themselves Slaves of Sin are swarming over the country, flagellating themselves and others, all for the glory of God.

Jons: Do they really whip themselves?

Painter: Yes, it's a terrible sight. I crawl into a ditch and hide when they pass by.

Jons: Do you have any brandy? I've been drinking water all day and it's made me as thirsty as a camel in the desert.

Painter: I think I frightened you after all.

Jons *sits down with the* Painter, *who produces a jug of brandy.*

The Knight *is kneeling before a small altar. It is dark and quiet around him. The air is cool and musty. Pictures of saints look down on him with stony eyes. Christ's face is turned upwards, His mouth open as if in a cry of anguish. On the ceiling beam there is a representation of a hideous devil spying on a miserable human being. The* Knight *hears a sound from the confession booth and approaches it. The face of* Death *appears behind the grille for an instant, but the* Knight *doesn't see him.*

Knight: I want to talk to you as openly as I can, but my heart is empty.

Death *doesn't answer.*

Knight: The emptiness is a mirror turned towards my own face. I see myself in it, and I am filled with fear and disgust.

Death *doesn't answer.*

Knight: Through my indifference to my fellow men, I have isolated myself from their company. Now I live in a world of phantoms. I am imprisoned in my dreams and fantasies.

Death: And yet you don't want to die.

Knight: Yes, I do.

DEATH : What are you waiting for?
KNIGHT : I want knowledge.
DEATH : You want guarantees?
KNIGHT : Call it whatever you like. Is it so cruelly inconceivable to grasp God with the senses? Why should He hide himself in a mist of half-spoken promises and unseen miracles?

  DEATH *doesn't answer.*

KNIGHT : How can we have faith in those who believe when we can't have faith in ourselves? What is going to happen to those of us who want to believe but aren't able to? And what is to become of those who neither want to nor are capable of believing?

  The KNIGHT *stops and waits for a reply, but no one speaks or answers him. There is complete silence.*

KNIGHT : Why can't I kill God within me? Why does He live on in this painful and humiliating way even though I curse Him and want to tear Him out of my heart? Why, in spite of everything, is He a baffling reality that I can't shake off? Do you hear me?
DEATH : Yes, I hear you.
KNIGHT : I want knowledge, not faith, not suppositions, but knowledge. I want God to stretch out His hand towards me, reveal Himself and speak to me.
DEATH : But He remains silent.
KNIGHT : I call out to Him in the dark but no one seems to be there.
DEATH : Perhaps no one is there.
KNIGHT : Then life is an outrageous horror. No one can live in the face of death, knowing that all is nothingness.
DEATH : Most people never reflect about either death or the futility of life.
KNIGHT : But one day they will have to stand at that last moment of life and look towards the darkness.
DEATH : When *that* day comes ...
KNIGHT : In our fear, we make an image, and that image we call God.

DEATH: You are worrying...
KNIGHT: Death visited me this morning. We are playing chess together. This reprieve gives me the chance to arrange an urgent matter.
DEATH: What matter is that?
KNIGHT: My life has been a futile pursuit, a wandering, a great deal of talk without meaning. I feel no bitterness or self-reproach because the lives of most people are very much like this. But I will use my reprieve for one meaningful deed.
DEATH: Is that why you are playing chess with Death?
KNIGHT: He is a clever opponent, but up to now I haven't lost a single man.
DEATH: How will you outwit Death in your game?
KNIGHT: I use a combination of the bishop and the knight which he hasn't yet discovered. In the next move I'll shatter one of his flanks.
DEATH: I'll remember that.

DEATH shows his face at the grille of the confession booth for a moment but disappears instantly.

KNIGHT: You've tricked and cheated me! But we'll meet again, and I'll find a way.
DEATH *invisible*: We'll meet at the inn, and there we'll continue playing.

The KNIGHT raises his hand and looks at it in the sunlight which comes through the tiny window.

KNIGHT: This is my hand. I can move it, feel the blood pulsing through it. The sun is still high in the sky and I, Antonius Block, am playing chess with Death.

He makes a fist of his hand and lifts it to his temple.

Meanwhile, JONS and the PAINTER have got drunk and are talking animatedly together.

JONS: Me and my master have been abroad and have just come home. Do you understand, you little pictor?
PAINTER: The Crusade.
JONS *drunk*: Precisely. For ten years we sat in the Holy Land

and let snakes bite us, flies sting us, wild animals eat us, heathens butcher us, the wine poison us, the women give us lice, the lice devour us, the fevers rot us, all for the Glory of God. Our crusade was such madness that only a real idealist could have thought it up. But what you said about the plague was horrible.

PAINTER: It's worse than that.

JONS: Ah me. No matter which way you turn, you have your rump behind you. That's the truth.

PAINTER: The rump behind you, the rump behind you — there's a profound truth.

JONS paints a small figure which is supposed to represent himself.

JONS: This is squire Jöns. He grins at Death, mocks the Lord, laughs at himself and leers at the girls. His world is a Jöns-world, believable only to himself, ridiculous to all including himself, meaningless to Heaven and of no interest to Hell.

The KNIGHT walks by, calls to his squire and goes out into the bright sunshine. JONS manages to get himself down from the scaffolding.

Outside the church, four soldiers and a monk are in the process of putting a woman in the stocks. Her face is pale and child-like, her head has been shaved, and her knuckles are bloody and broken. Her eyes are wide open, yet she doesn't appear to be fully conscious.

JONS and the KNIGHT stop and watch in silence. The soldiers are working quickly and skilfully, but they seem frightened and dejected. The monk mumbles from a small book. One of the soldiers picks up a wooden bucket and with his hand begins to smear a bloody paste on the wall of the church and around the woman. JONS holds his nose.

JONS: That soup of yours has a hell of a stink. What is it good for?

SOLDIER: She has had carnal intercourse with the Evil One.

He whispers this with a horrified face and continues to

splash the sticky mess on the wall.
JONS : And now she's in the stocks.
SOLDIER : She will be burned tomorrow morning at the parish boundary. But we have to keep the Devil away from the rest of us.
JONS *holding his nose* : And you do that with this stinking mess?
SOLDIER : It's the best remedy : blood mixed with the bile of a big black dog. The Devil can't stand the smell.
JONS : Neither can I.

JONS walks over towards the horses. The KNIGHT stands for a few moments looking at the young girl. She is almost a child. Slowly she turns her eyes towards him.

KNIGHT : Have you seen the Devil?

The MONK stops reading and raises his head.

MONK : You must not talk to her.
KNIGHT : Can that be so dangerous?
MONK : I don't know, but she is believed to have caused the pestilence with which we are afflicted.
KNIGHT : I understand.

He nods resignedly and walks away. The young woman starts to moan as though she were having a horrible nightmare. The sound of her cries follows the two riders for a considerable distance down the road.

The sun stands high in the sky, like a red ball of fire. The waterskin is empty and JONS looks for a well where he can fill it.

They approach a group of peasant cottages at the edge of the forest. JONS ties up the horses, slings the skin over his shoulder and walks along the path towards the nearest cottage. As always, his movements are light and almost soundless. The door to the cottage is open. He stops outside, but when no one appears he enters. It is very dark inside and his foot touches a soft object. He looks down. Beside the whitewashed fireplace, a woman is

lying with her face to the ground.
At the sound of approaching steps, JONS *quickly hides behind the door. A man comes down a ladder from the loft. He is broad and thick-set. His eyes are black and his face is pale and puffy. His clothes are well cut but dirty and in rags. He carries a cloth sack. Looking around, he goes into the inner room, bends over the bed, tucks something into the bag, slinks along the walls, looking on the shelves, finds something else which he tucks in his bag.*
Slowly he re-enters the outer room, bends over the dead woman and carefully slips a ring from her finger. At that moment a young woman comes through the door. She stops and stares at the stranger.

RAVAL: Why do you look so surprised? I steal from the dead. These days it's quite a lucrative enterprise.

The GIRL *makes a movement as if to run away.*

RAVEL: You're thinking of running to the village and telling. That wouldn't serve any purpose. Each of us has to save his own skin. It's as simple as that.

GIRL: Don't touch me.

RAVAL: Don't try to scream. There's no one around to hear you, neither God nor man.

Slowly he closes the door behind the GIRL. *The stuffy room is now in almost total darkness. But* JONS *becomes clearly visible.*

JONS: I recognise you, although it's a long time since we met. Your name is Raval, from the theological college at Roskilde. You are Dr. Mirabilis, Coelestis et Diabilis.

RAVAL *smiles uneasily and looks around.*

JONS: Am I not right?

The GIRL *stands immobile.*

JONS: You were the one who, ten years ago, convinced my master of the necessity to join a better-class crusade to the Holy Land.

RAVAL *looks around.*

Jons: You look uncomfortable. Do you have a stomach-ache?
   Raval *smiles anxiously.*
Jons: When I see you, I suddenly understand the meaning of these ten years, which previously seemed to me such a waste. Our life was too good and we were too satisfied with ourselves. The Lord wanted to punish us for our complacency. That is why He sent you to spew out your holy venom and poison the knight.
Raval: I acted in good faith.
Jons: But now you know better, don't you? Because now you have turned into a thief. A more fitting and rewarding occupation for scoundrels. Isn't that so?
   With a quick movement he knocks the knife out of Raval's *hand, gives him a kick so that he falls on the floor and is about to finish him off. Suddenly the* Girl *screams.* Jons *stops and makes a gesture of generosity with his hand.*
Jons: By all means. I'm not bloodthirsty.
   He bends over Raval.
Raval: Don't beat me.
Jons: I don't have the heart to touch you, Doctor. But remember this: the next time we meet, I'll brand your face the way one does with thieves. *He rises.* What I really came for is to get my waterskin filled.
Girl: We have a deep well with cool, fresh water. Come, I'll show you.
   They walk out of the house. Raval *lies still for a few moments, then he rises slowly and looks around. When no one is in sight, he takes his bag and steals away.*
   Jons *quenches his thirst and fills his bag with water. The* Girl *helps him.*
Jons: Jöns is my name. I am a pleasant and talkative young man who has never had anything but kind thoughts and has only done beautiful and noble deeds. I'm kindest of all to young women. With them, there is no limit to my kindness.
   He embraces her and tries to kiss her, but she holds her-

self back. Almost immediately he loses interest, hoists the waterbag on his shoulder and pats the GIRL *on the cheek.*

JONS : Goodbye, my girl. I could very well have raped you, but between you and me, I'm tired of that kind of love. It runs a little dry in the end.

He laughs kindly and walks away from her. When he has walked a short distance he turns; the GIRL *is still there.*

JONS : Now that I think of it, I will need a housekeeper. Can you prepare good food? *The* GIRL *nods.* As far as I know, I'm still a married man, but I have high hopes that my wife is dead by now. That's why I need a housekeeper. *The* GIRL *doesn't answer but gets up.* The devil with it! Come along and don't stand there staring. I've saved your life, so you owe me a great deal.

She begins walking towards him, her head bent. He doesn't wait for her but walks towards the KNIGHT, *who patiently awaits his squire.*

The Embarrassment Inn lies in the eastern section of the province. The plague has not yet reached this area on its way along the coast.

The actors have placed their wagon under a tree in the yard of the inn. Dressed in colourful costumes, they perform a farce.

The spectators watch the performance, commenting on it noisily. There are merchants with fat, beer-sweaty faces, apprentices and journeymen, farmhands and milk-maids. A whole flock of children perch in the trees around the wagon.

The KNIGHT *and his squire have sat down in the shadow of a wall. They drink beer and doze in the midday heat.*
The GIRL *from the deserted village sleeps at* JONS'S *side.*
SKAT *beats the drums,* JOF *blows the flute,* MIA *performs a gay and lively dance. They perspire under the hot white*

sun. When they have finished SKAT *comes forward and bows.*
SKAT: Noble ladies and gentlemen, I thank you for your interest. Please remain standing a little longer, or sit on the ground, because we are now going to perform a tragedia about an unfaithful wife, her jealous husband, and the handsome lover — that's me.
  MIA *and* JOF *have quickly changed costumes and again step out on the stage. They bow to the public.*
SKAT: Here is the husband. Here is the wife. If you'll shut up over there, you'll see something splendid. As I said, I play the lover and I haven't entered yet. That's why I'm going to hide behind the curtain for the time being. *He wipes the sweat from his forehead.* It's damned hot. I think we'll have a thunderstorm.
  He places his leg in front of JOF *as if to trip him, raises* MIA'S *skirt, makes a face as if he could see all the wonders of the world underneath it, and disappears behind the gaudily patched curtains.*
  SKAT *is very handsome, now that he can see himself in the reflection of a tin washbowl. His hair is tightly curled, his eyebrows are beautifully bushy, glittering earrings vie for equal attention with his teeth, and his cheeks are flushed rose red.*
  He sits out in back on the tailboard of the wagon, dangling his legs and whistling to himself.
  In the meantime JOF *and* MIA *play their tragedy; it is not, however, received with great acclaim.*
  SKAT *suddenly discovers that someone is watching him as he gazes contentedly into the tin bowl. A woman stands there, stately in both height and volume.*
  SKAT *frowns, toys with his small dagger and occasionally throws a roguish but fiery glance at the beautiful visitor. She suddenly discovers that one of her shoes doesn't quite fit. She leans down to fix it and in doing so allows her generous bosom to burst out of its prison — no more*

than honour and chastity allow, but still enough so that the actor with his experienced eye immediately sees that there are ample rewards to be had here.

Now she comes a little closer, kneels down and opens a bundle containing several dainty morsels and a skin filled with red wine. JONAS SKAT manages not to fall off the wagon in his excitement. Standing on the steps of the wagon, he supports himself against a nearby tree, crosses his legs and bows.

The woman quietly bites into a chicken leg dripping with fat. At this moment the actor is stricken by a radiant glance full of lustful appetites.

When he sees this look, SKAT makes an instantaneous decision, jumps down from the wagon and kneels in front of the blushing damsel.

She becomes weak and faint from his nearness, looks at him with a glassy glance and breathes heavily. SKAT doesn't neglect to press kisses on her small, chubby hands. The sun shines brightly and small birds make noises in the bushes.

Now she is forced to sit back; her legs seem unwilling to support her any longer. Bewildered, she singles out another chicken leg from the large sack of food and holds it up in front of SKAT with an appealing and triumphant expression, as if it were her maidenhood being offered as a prize.

SKAT hesitates momentarily, but he is still the strategist. He lets the chicken leg fall to the grass, and murmurs in the woman's rosy ear.

His words seem to please her. She puts her arms around the actor's neck and pulls him to her with such fierceness that both of them lose their balance and tumble down on the soft grass. The small birds take to their wings with frightened shrieks.

JOF stands in the hot sun with a flickering lantern in

his hand. MIA *pretends to be asleep on a bench which has been pulled forward on the stage.*
JOF : Night and moonlight now prevail
Here sleeps my wife so frail . . .
VOICE FROM THE PUBLIC : Does she snore?
JOF : May I point out that this is a tragedy, and in tragedies one doesn't snore.
VOICE FROM THE PUBLIC : I think she should snore anyhow.
This opinion causes mirth in the audience. JOF *becomes slightly confused and goes out of character, but* MIA *keeps her head and begins snoring.*
JOF : Night and moonlight now prevail.
There snores — I mean sleeps — my wife so frail.
Jealous I am, as never before,
I hide myself behind this door.
Faithful is she
To her lover — not me.
He soon comes a-stealing
To awaken her lusty feeling.
I shall now kill him dead
For cuckolding me in my bed.
There he comes in the moonlight,
His white legs shining bright.
Quiet as a mouse, here I'll lie,
Tell him not that he's about to die.
JOF *hides himself.* MIA *immediately ends her snoring and sits up, looking to the left.*
MIA : Look, there he comes in the night
My lover, my heart's delight.
She becomes silent and looks wide-eyed in front of her.
The mood in the yard in front of the inn has, up to now, been rather lighthearted despite the heat.
Now a rapid change occurs. People who had been laughing and chattering fall silent. Their faces seem to pale under their sunbrowned skins, the children stop their games and stand with gaping mouths and frightened eyes.

JOF *steps out in front of the curtain. His painted face bears an expression of horror.* MIA *has risen with* MIKAEL *in her arms. Some of the women in the yard have fallen on their knees, others hide their faces, many begin to mutter half-forgotten prayers.*
All have turned their faces towards the white road. Now a shrill song is heard. It is frenzied, almost a scream.
A crucified Christ sways above the hilltop.
The cross-bearers soon come into sight. They are Dominican monks, their hoods pulled down over their faces. More and more of them follow, carrying litters with heavy coffins or clutching holy relics, their hands stretched out spasmodically. The dust wells up around their black hoods; the censers sway and emit a thick, ashen smoke which smells of rancid herbs.
After the line of monks comes another procession. It is a column of men, boys, old men, women, girls, children. All of them have steel-edged scourges in their hands with which they whip themselves and each other, howling ecstatically. They twist in pain; their eyes bulge wildly; their lips are gnawed to shreds and dripping with foam. They have been seized by madness. They bite their own hands and arms, whip each other in violent, almost rhythmic outbursts. Throughout it all the shrill song howls from their bursting throats. Many sway and fall, lift themselves up again, support each other and help each other to intensify the scourging.
Now the procession pauses at the crossroads in front of the inn. The monks fall on their knees, hiding their faces with clenched hands, arms pressed tightly together. Their song never stops. The Christ figure on its timbered cross is raised above the heads of the crowd. It is not Christ triumphant, but the suffering Jesus with the sores, the blood, the hammered nails and the face in convulsive pain. The Son of God, nailed on the wood of the cross, suffering scorn and shame.

The penitents have now sunk down in the dirt of the road. They collapse where they stood like slaughtered cattle. Their screams rise with the song of the monks, through misty clouds of incense, towards the white fire of the sun.

A large square monk rises from his knees and reveals his face, which is red-brown from the sun. His eyes glitter; his voice is thick with impotent scorn.

MONK: God has sentenced us to punishment. We shall all perish in the black death. You, standing there like gaping cattle, you who sit there in your glutted complacency, do you know that this may be your last hour? Death stands right behind you. I can see how his crown gleams in the sun. His scythe flashes as he raises it above your heads. Which one of you shall he strike first? You there, who stand staring like a goat, will your mouth be twisted into the last unfinished gasp before nightfall? And you, woman, who bloom with life and self-satisfaction, will you pale and become extinguished before the morning dawns? You back there, with your swollen nose and stupid grin, do you have another year left to dirty the earth with your refuse? Do you know, you insensible fools, that you shall die today or tomorrow, or the next day, because all of you have been sentenced? Do you hear what I say? Do you hear the word? You have been sentenced, sentenced!

The MONK *falls silent, looking around with a bitter face and a cold, scornful glance. Now he clenches his hands, straddles the ground and turns his face upwards.*

MONK: Lord have mercy on us in our humiliation! Don't turn your face from us in loathing and contempt, but be merciful to us for the sake of your son, Jesus Christ.

He makes the sign of the cross over the crowd and then begins a new song in a strong voice. The monks rise and join in the song. As if driven by some superhuman force, the penitents begin to whip themselves again, still wailing and moaning.

The procession continues. New members have joined the

rear of the column; others who were unable to go on lie weeping in the dust of the road.

Jons the squire drinks his beer.

Jons: This damned ranting about doom. Is that food for the minds of modern people? Do they really expect us to take them seriously?

The Knight grins tiredly.

Jons: Yes, now you grin at me, my lord. But allow me to point out that I've either read, heard or experienced most of the tales which we people tell each other.

Knight *yawns*: Yes, yes.

Jons: Even the ghost stories about God the Father, the angels, Jesus Christ and the Holy Ghost — all these I've accepted without too much emotion.

He leans down over the Girl as she crouches at his feet and pats her on the head. The Knight drinks his beer silently.

Jons *contentedly*: My little stomach is my world, my head is my eternity, and my hands, two wonderful suns. My legs are time's damned pendulums, and my dirty feet are two splendid starting points for my philosophy. Everything is worth precisely as much as a belch, the only difference being that a belch is more satisfying.

The beer mug is empty. Sighing, Jons gets to his feet. The Girl follows him like a shadow.

In the yard he meets a large man with a sooty face and a dark expression. He stops Jons with a roar.

Jons: What are you screaming about?

Plog: I am Plog, the smith, and you are the squire Jöns.

Jons: That's possible.

Plog: Have you seen my wife?

Jons: No, I haven't. But if I had seen her and she looked like you, I'd quickly forget that I'd seen her.

Plog: Well, in that case you haven't seen her.

Jons: Maybe she's run off.

Plog: Do you know anything?

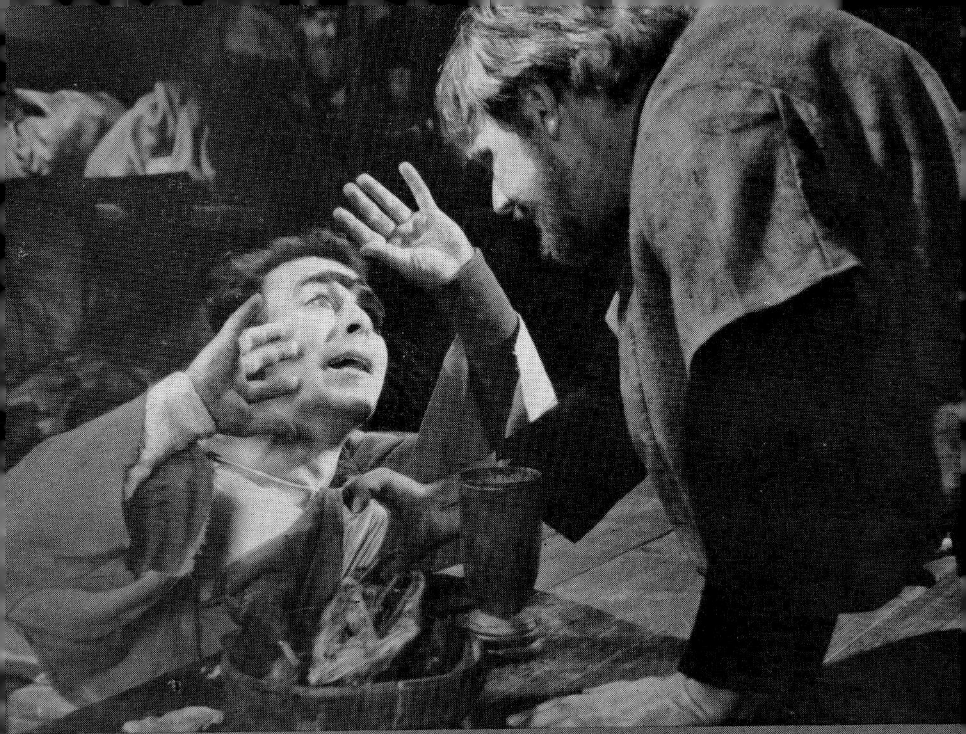

JONS: I know quite a lot, but not about your wife. Go to the inn. Maybe they can help you.

The SMITH sighs sadly and goes inside.

The inn is very small and full of people eating and drinking to forget their newly aroused fears of eternity. In the open fireplace a roasting pig turns on an iron spit. The sun shines outside the casement window, its sharp rays piercing the darkness of the room, which is thick with fumes and perspiration.

MERCHANT: Yes, it's true! The plague is spreading along the west coast. People are dying like flies. Usually business would be good at this time of year, but, damn it, I've still got my whole stock unsold.

WOMAN: They speak of the judgment day. And all these omens are terrible. Worms, chopped-off hands and other monstrosities began pouring out of an old woman, and down in the village another woman gave birth to a calf's head.

OLD MAN: The day of judgment. Imagine.

FARMER: It hasn't rained here for a month. We'll surely lose our crops.

MERCHANT: And people are acting crazy, I'd say. They flee the country and carry the plague with them wherever they go.

OLD MAN: The day of judgment. Just think, just think!

FARMER: If it's as they say, I suppose a person should look after his house and try to enjoy life as long as he can.

WOMAN: But there have been other things too, such things that can't even be spoken of. *Whispers.* Things that mustn't be named — but the priests say that the woman carries it between her legs and that's why she must cleanse herself.

OLD MAN: Judgment day. And the Riders of the Apocalypse stand at the bend in the village road. I imagine they'll come on judgment night, at sundown.

WOMAN: There are many who have purged themselves with fire and died from it, but the priests say that it's better to die pure than to live for hell.

MERCHANT: This is the end, yes, it is. No one says it out loud, but all of us know that it's the end. And people are going mad from fear.
FARMER: So you're afraid too.
MERCHANT: Of course I'm afraid.
OLD MAN: The judgment day becomes night, and the angels descend and the graves open. It will be terrible to see.

They whisper in low tones and sit close to each other.

PLOG, *the smith, shoves his way into a place next to* JOF, *who is still dressed in his costume. Opposite him sits* RAVAL, *leaning slightly forward, his face perspiring heavily.* RAVAL *rolls an armlet out on the table.*

RAVAL: Do you want this armlet? You can have it cheap.
JOF: I can't afford it.
RAVAL: It's real silver.
JOF: It's nice. But it's surely too expensive for me.
PLOG: Excuse me, but has anyone here seen my wife?
JOF: Has she disappeared?
PLOG: They say she's run away.
JOF: Has she deserted you?
PLOG: With an actor.
JOF: An actor! If she's got such bad taste, then I think you should let her go.
PLOG: You're right. My first thought, of course, was to kill her.
JOF: Oh. But to murder her, that's a terrible thing to do.
PLOG: I'm also going to kill the actor.
JOF: The actor?
PLOG: Of course, the one she eloped with.
JOF: What has he done to deserve that?
PLOG: Are you stupid?
JOF: The actor! Now I understand. There are too many of them, so even if he hasn't done anything in particular you ought to kill him merely because he's an actor.
PLOG: You see, my wife has always been interested in the

tricks of the theatre.
JOF: And that turned out to be her misfortune.
PLOG: Her misfortune, but not mine, because a person who's born unfortunate can hardly suffer from any further misfortune. Isn't that true?
> *Now* RAVAL *enters the discussion. He is slightly drunk and his voice is shrill and evil.*

RAVAL: Listen, you! You sit there and lie to the smith.
JOF: I! A liar!
RAVAL: You're an actor too and it's probably your partner who's run off with Plog's old lady.
PLOG: Are you an actor too?
JOF: An actor! Me! I wouldn't quite call myself that!
RAVAL: We ought to kill you; it's only logical.
JOF *laughs*: You're really funny.
RAVAL: How strange — you've turned pale. Have you anything on your conscience?
JOF: You're funny. Don't you think he's funny? *To Plog.* Oh, you don't.
RAVAL: Maybe we should mark you up a little with a knife, like they do petty scoundrels of your kind.
> PLOG *bangs his hands down on the table so that the dishes jump. He gets up.*

PLOG *shouting*: What have you done with my wife?
> *The room becomes silent.* JOF *looks around, but there is no exit, no way to escape. He puts his hands on the table. Suddenly a knife flashes through the air and sinks into the table top between his fingers.*
>
> JOF *snatches away his hands and raises his head. He looks half surprised, as if the truth had just become apparent to him.*

JOF: Do you want to hurt me? Why? Have I provoked someone, or got in the way? I'll leave right now and never come back.
> JOF *looks from one face to another, but no one seems ready to help him or come to his defence.*

RAVAL: Get up so everyone can hear you. Talk louder.
> *Trembling, JOF rises. He opens his mouth as if to say something, but not a word comes out.*

RAVAL: Stand on your head so that we can see how good an actor you are.
> *JOF gets up on the table and stands on his head. A hand pushes him forward so that he collapses on the floor. PLOG rises, pulls him to his feet with one hand.*

PLOG *shouts*: What have you done with my wife?
> *PLOG beats him so furiously that JOF flies across the table. RAVAL leans over him.*

RAVAL: Don't lie there moaning. Get up and dance.

JOF: I don't want to. I can't.

RAVAL: Show us how you imitate a bear.

JOF: I can't play a bear.

RAVAL: Let's see if you can't after all.
> *RAVAL prods JOF lightly with the knife point. JOF gets up with cold sweat on his cheeks and forehead, frightened half to death. He begins to jump and hop on top of the tables, swinging his arms and legs and making grotesque faces. Some laugh, but most of the people sit silently. JOF gasps as if his lungs were about to burst. He sinks to his knees, and someone pours beer over him.*

RAVAL: Up again! Be a good bear.

JOF: I haven't done any harm. I haven't got the strength to play a bear any more.
> *At that moment the door opens and JONS enters. JOF sees his chance and steals out. RAVAL intends to follow him, but suddenly stops. JONS and RAVAL look at each other.*

JONS: Do you remember what I was going to do to you if we met again?
> *RAVAL steps back without speaking.*

JONS: I'm a man who keeps his word.
> *JONS raises his knife and cuts RAVAL from forehead to cheek. RAVAL staggers towards the wall.*

The hot day has become night. Singing and howling can be heard from the inn. In a hollow near the forest, the light still lingers. Hidden in the grass and the shrubbery, nightingales sing and their voices echo through the stillness.

The players' wagon stands in a small ravine, and not far away the horse grazes on the dry grass. MIA *has sat down in front of the wagon with her son in her arms. They play together and laugh happily.*

Now a soft gleam of light strokes the hilltops, a last reflection from the red clouds over the sea.

Not far from the wagon, the KNIGHT *sits crouched over his chess game. He lifts his head.*

The evening light moves across the heavy wagon wheels, across the woman and the child.

The KNIGHT *gets up.*

MIA *sees him and smiles. She holds up her struggling son, as if to amuse the* KNIGHT.

KNIGHT : What's his name?
MIA : Mikael.
KNIGHT : How old is he?
MIA : Oh, he'll soon be two.
KNIGHT : He's big for his age.
MIA : Do you think so? Yes, I guess he's rather big.
   She puts the child down on the ground and half rises to shake out her red skirt. When she sits down again, the KNIGHT *steps closer.*
KNIGHT : You played some kind of show this afternoon.
MIA : Did you think it was bad?
KNIGHT : You are more beautiful now without your face painted, and this gown is more becoming.
MIA : You see, Jonas Skat has run off and left us, so we're in real trouble now.
KNIGHT : Is that your husband?
MIA *laughs*: Jonas! The other man is my husband. His name is Jof.

KNIGHT: Oh, that one.
MIA: And now there's only him and me. We'll have to start doing tricks again and that's more trouble than it's worth.
KNIGHT: Do you do tricks also?
MIA: We certainly do. And Jof is a very skilful juggler.
KNIGHT: Is Mikael going to be an acrobat?
MIA: Jof wants him to be.
KNIGHT: But you don't.
MIA: I don't know *Smiling*. Perhaps he'll become a knight.
KNIGHT: Let me assure you, that's no pleasure either.
MIA: No, you don't look so happy.
KNIGHT: No.
MIA: Are you tired?
KNIGHT: Yes.
MIA: Why?
KNIGHT: I have dull company.
MIA: Do you mean your squire?
KNIGHT: No, not him.
MIA: Who do you mean, then?
KNIGHT: Myself.
MIA: I understand.
KNIGHT: Do you, really?
MIA: Yes, I understand rather well. I have often wondered why people torture themselves as often as they can. Isn't that so?

She nods energetically and the KNIGHT *smiles seriously. Now the shrieks and the noise from the inn become louder. Black figures flicker across the grass mound. Someone collapses, gets up and runs. It is* JOF. MIA *stretches out her arms and receives him. He holds his hands in front of his face, moaning like a child, and his body sways. He kneels.* MIA *holds him close to her and sprinkles him with small, anxious questions:* What have you done? How are you? What is it? Does it hurt? What can I do? Have they been cruel to you? *She runs for a rag, which she dips in water, and carefully bathes her husband's*

    dirty, bloody face.
    Eventually a rather sorrowful visage emerges. Blood runs from a bruise on his forehead and his nose, and a tooth has been loosened, but otherwise JOF *seems unhurt.*
JOF: Ouch, it hurts.
MIA: Why did you have to go there? And of course you drank.
    MIA'S *anxiety has been replaced by a mild anger. She pats him a little harder than necessary.*
JOF: Ouch! I didn't drink anything.
MIA: Then I suppose you were boasting about the angels and devils you consort with. People don't like someone who has too many ideas and fantasies.
JOF: I swear to you that I didn't say a word about angels.
MIA: You were, of course, busy singing and dancing. You can never stop being an actor. People also become angry at that, and you know it.
    JOF *doesn't answer but searches for the armlet. He holds it up in front of* MIA *with an injured expression.*
JOF: Look what I bought for you.
MIA: You couldn't afford it.
JOF *angry*: But I got it anyhow.
    The armlet glitters faintly in the twilight. MIA *now pulls it across her wrist. They look at it in silence, and their faces soften. They look at each other, touch each other's hands.* JOF *puts his head against* MIA'S *shoulder and sighs.*
JOF: Oh, how they beat me.
MIA: Why didn't you beat them back?
JOF: I only become frightened and angry. I never get a chance to hit back. I can get angry, you know that. I roared like a lion.
MIA: Were they frightened?
JOF: No, they just laughed.
    Their son MIKAEL *crawls over to them.* JOF *lies down on the ground and pulls his son on top of him.* MIA *gets*

down on her hands and knees and playfully sniffs at MIKAEL.

MIA: Do you notice how good he smells?

JOF: And he is so compact to hold. You're a sturdy one. A real acrobat's body.

He lifts MIKAEL *up and holds him by the legs.* MIA *looks up suddenly, remembering the knight's presence.*

MIA: Yes, this is my husband, Jof.

JOF: Good evening.

KNIGHT: Good evening.

JOF *becomes a little embarrassed and rises. All three of them look at one another silently.*

KNIGHT: I have just told your wife that you have a splendid son. He'll bring great joy to you.

JOF: Yes, he's fine.

They become silent again.

JOF: Have we nothing to offer the knight, Mia?

KNIGHT: Thank you, I don't want anything.

MIA *housewifely*: I picked a basket of wild strawberries this afternoon. And we have a drop of milk fresh from a cow . . .

JOF: . . . that we were *allowed* to milk. So, if you would like to partake of this humble fare, it would be a great honour.

MIA: Please be seated and I'll bring the food.

They sit down. MIA *disappears with* MIKAEL.

KNIGHT: Where are you going next?

JOF: Up to the saints' feast at Elsinore.

KNIGHT: I wouldn't advise you to go there.

JOF: Why not, if I may ask?

KNIGHT: The plague has spread in that direction, following the coast line south. It's said that people are dying by the tens of thousands.

JOF: Really! Well, sometimes life is a little hard.

KNIGHT: May I suggest . . . JOF *looks at him, surprised* . . . that you follow me through the forest tonight and stay at my home if you like. Or go along the east coast. You'll probably be safer there.

> MIA *has returned with a bowl of wild strawberries and the milk, places it between them and gives each of them a spoon.*

JOF: I wish you good appetite.

KNIGHT: I humbly thank you.

MIA: These are wild strawberries from the forest. I have never seen such large ones. They grow up there on the hillside. Notice how they smell!

> *She points with a spoon and smiles. The* KNIGHT *nods, as if he were pondering some profound thought.* JOF *eats heartily.*

JOF: Your suggestion is good, but I must think it over.

MIA: It might be wise to have company going through the forest. It's said to be full of trolls and ghosts and bandits. That's what I've heard.

JOF *staunchly*: Yes, I'd say that it's not a bad idea, but I have to think about it. Now that Skat has left, I am responsible for the troupe. After all, I have become director of the whole company.

MIA *mimics*: After all, I have become director of the whole company.

> JONS *comes walking slowly down the hill, closely followed by the* GIRL. MIA *points with her spoon.*

MIA: Do you want some strawberries?

JOF: This man saved my life. Sit down, my friend, and let us be together.

MIA *stretches herself*: Oh, how nice this is.

KNIGHT: For a short while.

MIA: Nearly always. One day is like another. There is nothing strange about that. The summer, of course, is better than the winter, because in summer you don't have to be cold. But spring is best of all.

JOF: I have written a poem about the spring. Perhaps you'd like to hear it. I'll run and get my lyre. *He sprints towards the wagon.*

MIA: Not now, Jof. Our guests may not be amused by your songs.
JONS *politely*: By all means. I write little songs myself. For example, I know a very funny song about a wanton fish which I doubt that you've heard yet.
   The KNIGHT *looks at him.*
JONS: You'll not get to hear it either. There are persons here who don't appreciate my art and I don't want to upset anyone. I'm a sensitive soul.
   JOF *has come out with his lyre, sits on a small, gaudy box and plucks at the instrument, humming quietly, searching for his melody.* JONS *yawns and lies down.*
KNIGHT: People are troubled by so much.
MIA: It's always better when one is two. Have you no one of your own?
KNIGHT: Yes, I think I had someone.
MIA: And what is she doing now?
KNIGHT: I don't know.
MIA: You look so solemn. Was she your beloved?
KNIGHT: We were newly married and we played together. We laughed a great deal. I wrote songs to her eyes, to her nose, to her beautiful little ears. We went hunting together and at night we danced. The house was full of life . . .
MIA: Do you want some more strawberries?
KNIGHT *shakes his head*: Faith is a torment, did you know that? It is like loving someone who is out there in the darkness but never appears, no matter how loudly you call.
MIA: I don't understand what you mean.
KNIGHT: Everything I've said seems meaningless and unreal while I sit here with you and your husband. How unimportant it all becomes suddenly.
   He takes the bowl of milk in his hand and drinks deeply from it several times. Then he carefully puts it down and looks up, smiling.
MIA: Now you don't look so solemn.
KNIGHT: I shall remember this moment. The silence, the

twilight, the bowls of strawberries and milk, your faces in the evening light. Mikael sleeping, Jof with his lyre. I'll try to remember what we have talked about. I'll carry this memory between my hands as carefully as if it were a bowl filled to the brim with fresh milk. *He turns his face away and looks out towards the sea and the colourless grey sky.* And it will be an adequate sign — it will be enough for me.

He rises, nods to the others and walks down towards the forest. JOF *continues to play on his lyre.* MIA *stretches out on the grass.*

The KNIGHT *picks up his chess game and carries it towards the beach. It is quiet and deserted; the sea is still.*

DEATH: I have been waiting for you.

KNIGHT: Pardon me. I was detained for a few moments. Because I revealed my tactics to you, I'm in retreat. It's your move.

DEATH: Why do you look so satisfied?

KNIGHT: That's my secret.

DEATH: Of course. Now I take your knight.

KNIGHT: You did the right thing.

DEATH: Have you tricked me?

KNIGHT: Of course. You fell right in the trap. Check!

DEATH: What are you laughing at?

KNIGHT: Don't worry about my laughter; save your king instead.

DEATH: You're rather arrogant.

KNIGHT: Our game amuses me.

DEATH: It's your move. Hurry up. I'm a little pressed for time.

KNIGHT: I understand that you've a lot to do, but you can't get out of our game. It takes time.

DEATH *is about to answer him but stops and leans over the board. The* KNIGHT *smiles.*

DEATH: Are you going to escort the juggler and his wife through the forest? Those whose names are Jof and Mia and

who have a small son?
KNIGHT: Why do you ask?
DEATH: Oh, no reason at all.

The KNIGHT *suddenly stops smiling.* DEATH *looks at him scornfully.*

Immediately after sundown, the little company gathers in the yard of the inn. There is the KNIGHT, JONS *and the* GIRL, JOF *and* MIA *in their wagon. Their son,* MIKAEL, *is already asleep.* JONAS SKAT *is still missing.*
JONS *goes into the inn to get provisions for the night journey and to have a last mug of beer. The inn is now empty and quiet except for a few farmhands and maidens who are eating their evening meal in a corner.*
At one of the small windows sits a lonely, hunched-over fellow, with a jug of brandy in his hands. His expression is very sad. Once in a while he is shaken by a gigantic sob. It is PLOG, *the smith, who sits there and whimpers.*
JONS: God in heaven, isn't this Plog, the smith?
PLOG: Good evening.
JONS: Are you sitting here snivelling in loneliness?
PLOG: Yes, yes, look at the smith. He moans like a rabbit.
JONS: If I were in your boots, I'd be happy to get rid of a wife in such an easy way.

JONS *pats the smith on the back, quenches his thirst with beer, and sits down by his side.*
PLOG: Are *you* married?
JONS: *I!* A hundred times and more. I can't keep count of all my wives any longer. But it's often that way when you're a travelling man.
PLOG: I can assure you that *one* wife is worse than a hundred, or else I've had worse luck than any poor wretch in this miserable world, which isn't impossible.
JONS: Yes, it's hell *with* women and hell *without* them. So, however you look at it, it's still best to kill them off while it's most amusing.

PLOG: Women's nagging, the shrieking of children and wet nappies, sharp nails and sharp words, blows and pokes, and the devil's aunt for a mother-in-law. And then, when one wants to sleep after a long day, there's a new song — tears, whining and moans loud enough to wake the dead.

 JONS *nods delightedly. He has drunk deeply and talks with an old woman's voice.*

JONS: Why don't you kiss me good night?
PLOG *in the same way*: Why don't you sing a song for me?
JONS: Why don't you love me the way you did when we first met?
PLOG: Why don't you look at my new shift?
JONS: You only turn your back and snore.
PLOG: Oh hell!
JONS: Oh hell. And now she's gone. Rejoice!
PLOG *furious*: I'll snip their noses with pliers, I'll bash in their chests with a small hammer, I'll tap their heads ever so lightly with a sledge.

 PLOG *begins to cry loudly and his whole body sways in an enormous attack of sorrow.* JONS *looks at him with interest.*

JONS: Look how he howls again.
PLOG: Maybe I love her.
JONS: So, maybe you love her! Then, you poor misguided ham shank, I'll tell you that love is another word for lust, plus lust, plus lust and a damn lot of cheating, falseness, lies and all kinds of other fooling around.
PLOG: Yes, but it hurts anyway.
JONS: Of course. Love is the blackest of all plagues, and if one could die of it, there would be some pleasure in love. But you almost always get over it.
PLOG: No, no, not me.
JONS: Yes, you too. There are only a couple of poor wretches who die of love once in a while. Love is as contagious as a cold in the nose. It eats away at your strength, your independence, your morale, if you have any. If everything is

imperfect in this imperfect world, love is most perfect in its perfect imperfection.

PLOG: You're happy, you with your oily words, and, besides, you believe your own drivel.

JONS: Believe! Who said that I believed it? But I love to give good advice. If you ask me for advice you'll get two pieces for the price of one, because after all I really am an educated man.

JONS gets up from the table and strokes his face with his hands. PLOG becomes very unhappy and grabs his belt.

PLOG: Listen, Jöns. May I go with you through the forest? I'm so lonely and don't want to go home because everyone will laugh at me.

JONS: Only if you don't whimper all the time, because in that case we'll all have to avoid you.

PLOG gets up and embraces JONS. Slightly drunk, the two new friends walk towards the door.

When they come out in the yard, JOF immediately catches sight of them, becomes angry and yells a warning to JONS.

JOF: Jöns! Watch out. That one wants to fight all the time. He's not quite sane.

JONS: Yes, but now he's just snivelling.

PLOG steps up to JOF, who blanches with fear. PLOG offers his hand.

PLOG: I'm really sorry if I hurt you. But I have such a hell of a temper, you know. Shake hands.

JOF gingerly proffers a frightened hand and gets it thoroughly shaken and squeezed. While JOF tries to straighten out his fingers, PLOG is seized by great good will and opens his arms.

PLOG: Come in my arms, little brother.

JOF: Thank you, thank you, perhaps later. But now we're really in a hurry.

JOF climbs up on the wagon seat quickly and clucks at the horse.

> The small company is on its way towards the forest and the night.
> It is dark in the forest.
> First comes the KNIGHT on his large horse. Then JOF and MIA follow, sitting close to each other in the juggler's wagon. MIA holds her son in her arms. JONS follows them with his heavily laden horse. He has the smith in tow. The GIRL sits on top of the load on the horse's back, hunched over as if asleep.
> The footsteps, the horses' heavy tramp on the soft path, the human breathing — yet it is quiet.
> Then the moon sails out of the clouds. The forest suddenly becomes alive with the night's unreality. The dazzling light pours through the thick foliage of the beech trees, a moving, quivering world of light and shadow.
> The wanderers stop. Their eyes are dark with anxiety and foreboding. Their faces are pale and unreal in the floating light. It is very quiet.

PLOG: Now the moon has come out of the clouds.
JONS: That's good. Now we can see the road better.
MIA: I don't like the moon tonight.
JOF: The trees stand so still.
JONS: That's because there's no wind.
PLOG: I guess he means that they stand *very* still.
JOF: It's completely quiet.
JONS: If one could hear a fox at least.
JOF: Or an owl.
JONS: Or a human voice besides one's own.
GIRL: They say it's dangerous to remain standing in moonlight.

> Suddenly, out of the silence and the dim light falling across the forest road, a ghostlike cart emerges.
> It is the WITCH being taken to the place where she will be burned. Next to her eight soldiers shuffle along tiredly, carrying their lances on their backs. The girl sits in

the cart, bound with iron chains around her throat and arms. She stares fixedly into the moonlight.
A black figure sits next to her, a monk with his hood pulled down over his head.

JONS : Where are you going?
SOLDIER : To the place of execution.
JONS : Yes, now I can see. It's the girl who has done it with the Black One. The witch?

The SOLDIER *nods sourly. Hesitantly, the travellers follow. The* KNIGHT *guides his horse over to the side of the cart. The* WITCH *seems to be half-conscious, but her eyes are wide open.*

KNIGHT : I see that they have hurt your hands.

The WITCH'S *pale, childish face turns towards the* KNIGHT *and she shakes her head.*

KNIGHT : I have a potion that will stop your pain.

She shakes her head again.

JONS : Why do you burn her at this time of night? People have so few diversions these days.
SOLDIER : Saints preserve us, be quiet! It's said that she brings the Devil with her wherever she goes.
JONS : You are eight brave men, then.
SOLDIER : Well, we've been paid. And this is a volunteer job.

The SOLDIER *speaks in whispers while glancing anxiously at the* WITCH.

KNIGHT *to the* WITCH : What's your name?
TYAN : My name is Tyan, my lord.
KNIGHT : How old are you?
TYAN : Fourteen, my lord.
KNIGHT : And is it true that you have been in league with the Devil?

TYAN *nods quietly and looks away. Now they arrive at the parish border. At the foot of the nearby hills lies a crossroads. The pyre has already been stacked in the centre of the forest clearing. The travellers remain there, hesitant and curious.*

The soldiers have tied up the cart horse and bring out two long wooden beams. They nail rungs across the beams so that it looks like a ladder. TYAN *will be bound to this like an eelskin stretched out to dry.*
The sound of the hammering echoes through the forest. The KNIGHT *has dismounted and walks closer to the cart. Again he tries to catch* TYAN'S *eyes, touches her very lightly as if to waken her.*
Slowly she turns her face towards him.

KNIGHT: They say that you have been in league with the Devil.

TYAN: Why do you ask?

KNIGHT: Not out of curiosity, but for very personal reasons. I too want to meet him.

TYAN: Why?

KNIGHT: I want to ask him about God. He, if anyone, must know.

TYAN: You can see him anytime.

KNIGHT: How?

TYAN: You must do as I tell you.

The KNIGHT *grips the wooden rail of the cart so tightly that his knuckles whiten.* TYAN *leans forward and joins her gaze with his.*

TYAN: Look into my eyes.

The KNIGHT *meets her gaze. They stare at each other for a long time.*

TYAN: What do you see? Do you see *him*?

KNIGHT: I see fear in your eyes, an empty, numb fear. But nothing else.

He falls silent. The soldiers work at the stakes; their hammering echoes in the forest.

TYAN: No one, nothing, no one?

KNIGHT *shakes his head*: No.

TYAN: Can't you see him behind your back?

KNIGHT *looks around*: No, there is no one there.

TYAN: But he is with me everywhere. I only have to stretch

out my hand and I can feel his hand. He is with me now too. The fire won't hurt me. He will protect me from everything evil.

KNIGHT: Has he told you this?

TYAN: I know it.

KNIGHT: Has he said it?

TYAN: I know it, I know it. You must see him somewhere, you must. The priests had no difficulty seeing him, nor did the soldiers. They are so afraid of him that they don't even dare touch me.

> The sounds of the hammers stops. The soldiers stand like black shadows rooted in the moss. They fumble with the chains and pull at the neck iron. TYAN moans weakly, as if she were far away.

KNIGHT: Why have you crushed her hands?

SOLDIER *surly*: We didn't do it.

KNIGHT: Who did?

SOLDIER: Ask the monk.

> The soldiers pull the iron and the chains. TYAN'S shaven head sways, gleaming in the moonlight. Her blackened mouth opens as if to scream, but no sound emerges.
> They take her down from the cart and lead her towards the ladder and the stake. The KNIGHT turns to the MONK, who remains seated in the cart.

KNIGHT: What have you done with the child?

> DEATH *turns around and looks at him.*

DEATH: Don't you ever stop asking questions?

KNIGHT: No, I'll never stop.

> The soldiers chain TYAN to the rungs of the ladder. She submits resignedly, moans weakly like an animal and tries to ease her body into position.
> When they have fastened her, they walk over to light the pyre. The KNIGHT steps up and leans over her.

JONS: For a moment I thought of killing the soldiers, but it would do no good. She's nearly dead already.

> One of the soldiers approaches. Thick smoke wells down

from the pyre and sweeps over the quiet shadows near the crossroads and the hill.
SOLDIER: I've told you to be careful. Don't go too close to her.
The KNIGHT doesn't heed this warning. He cups his hand, fills it with water from the skin and gives it to TYAN. Then he gives her a potion.
KNIGHT: Take this and it will stop the pain.
Smoke billows down over them and they begin to cough. The soldiers step forward and raise the ladder against a nearby fir tree. TYAN hangs there motionlessly, her eyes wide open.
The KNIGHT straightens up and stands immobile. JONS is behind him, his voice nearly choked with rage.
JONS: What does she see? Can you tell me?
KNIGHT *shakes his head*: She feels no more pain.
JONS: You don't answer my question. Who watches over that child? Is it the angels, or God, or the Devil, or only the emptiness? Emptiness, my lord!
KNIGHT: This cannot be.
JONS: Look at her eyes, my lord. Her poor brain has just made a discovery. Emptiness under the moon.
KNIGHT: No.
JONS: We stand powerless, our arms hanging at our sides, because we see what she sees, and our terror and hers are the same. *An outburst.* That poor little child. I can't stand it, I can't stand it . . .
His voice sticks in his throat and he suddenly walks away. The KNIGHT mounts his horse. The travellers depart from the crossroads. TYAN finally closes her eyes.

The forest is now very dark. The road winds between the trees. The wagon squeaks and rattles over stones and roots. A bird suddenly shrieks.
JOF *lifts his head and wakes up. He has been asleep with his arms around MIA's shoulders. The KNIGHT is sharply*

silhouetted against the tree trunks.
His silence makes him seem almost unreal.
Jons and Plog are slightly drunk and support each other. Suddenly Plog has to sit down. He puts his hands over his face and howls piteously.

Plog: Oh, now it came over me again!

Jons: Don't scream. What came over you?

Plog: My wife, damn it. She is so beautiful. She is so beautiful that she can't be described without the accompaniment of a lyre.

Jons: Now it starts again.

Plog: Her smile is like brandy. Her eyes like blackberries . . .

Plog searches for beautiful words. He gestures gropingly with his large hands.

Jons *sighs*: Get up, you tear-drenched pig. We'll lose the others.

Plog: Yes, of course, of course. Her nose is like a little pink potato; her behind is like a juicy pear — yes, the whole woman is like a strawberry patch. I can see her in front of me, with arms like wonderful cucumbers.

Jons: Saints almighty, stop! You're a very bad poet, despite the fact that you're drunk. And your vegetable garden bores me.

They walk across an open meadow. Here it is a little brighter and the moon shimmers behind a thin sky. Suddenly Plog points a large finger towards the edge of the forest.

Plog: Look there.

Jons: Do you see something?

Plog: There, over there!

Jons: I don't see anything.

Plog: Hang on to something, my friends. The hour is near! Who is that at the edge of the forest if not my own dearly beloved, with actor attached?

The two lovers discover Plog and it's too late. They

cannot retreat. SKAT *immediately takes to his heels.* PLOG *chases him, swinging his sledge and bellowing like a wild boar.*

For a few confusing moments the two rivals stumble among the stones and bushes in the grey gloom of the forest. The duel begins to look senseless, because both of them are equally frightened.

The travellers silently observe this confused performance. LISA *screams once in a while, more out of duty than out of impulse.*

SKAT *panting*: You miserable stubbleheaded bastard of seven scurvy bitches, if I were in your lousy rags I would be stricken with such eternal shame about my breath, my voice, my arms and legs — in short, about my whole body — that I would immediately rid nature of my own embarrassing self.

PLOG *angry*: Watch out, you perfumed slob, that I don't fart on you and immediately blow you down to the actor's own red-hot hell, where you can sit and recite monologues to each other until the dust comes out of the Devil's ears.

Then LISA *throws herself around her husband's neck.*

LISA: Forgive me, dear little husband, I'll never do it again. I am so sorry and you can't imagine how terribly that man over there betrayed me.

PLOG: I'll kill him anyway.

LISA: Yes, do that, just kill him. He isn't even a human being.

JONS: Hell, he's an actor.

LISA: He is only a false beard, false teeth, false smiles, rehearsed lines, and he's as empty as a jug. Just kill him.

LISA sobs with excitement and sorrow. PLOG looks around, a little confused. SKAT uses this opportunity. He pulls out a dagger and places the point against his breast.

SKAT: She's right. Just kill me. If you thought that I was going to apologize for being what I am, you are mistaken.

LISA: Look how sickening he is. How he makes a fool of

himself, how he puts on an act. Dear Plog, kill him.

SKAT: My friends, you have only to push, and my unreality will soon be transformed into a new, solid reality. An absolutely tangible corpse.

LISA: Do something then. Kill him.

PLOG *embarrassed*: He has to fight me, otherwise I can't kill him.

SKAT: Your life's thread now hands by a very ragged shred. Idiot, your day is short.

PLOG: You'll have to irritate me a little more to get me as angry as before.

> SKAT *looks at the travellers with a pained expression and then lifts his eyes towards the night sky.*

SKAT: I forgive all of you. Pray for me sometimes.

> SKAT *sinks the dagger into his breast and slowly falls to the ground. The travellers stand confused.* PLOG *rushes forward and begins to pull at* SKAT'S *hands.*

PLOG: Oh dear, dear, I didn't mean it that way! Look, there's no life left in him. I was beginning to like him, and in my opinion Lisa was much too spiteful.

> JOF *leans over his colleague.*

JOF: He's dead, totally, enormously dead. In fact, I've never seen such a dead actor.

LISA: Come on, let's go. This is nothing to mourn over. He has only himself to blame.

PLOG: And I have to be married to *her*.

JONS: We must go on.

> SKAT *lies in the grass and keeps the dagger pressed tightly to his breast. The travellers depart and soon they have disappeared into the dark forest on the other side of the meadow. When* SKAT *is sure that no one can see him, he sits up and lifts the dagger from his breast. It is a stage dagger with a blade that pushes into the handle.* SKAT *laughs to himself.*

SKAT: Now that was a good scene. I'm really a good actor. After all, why shouldn't I be a little pleased with myself?

But where shall I go? I'll wait until it becomes light and then I'll find the easiest way out of the forest. I'll climb up a tree for the time being so that no bears, wolves or ghosts can get at me.

He soon finds a likely tree and climbs up into its thick foliage. He sits down as comfortably as possible and reaches for his food pouch.

SKAT *yawns*: Tomorrow I'll find Jof and Mia and then we'll go to the saints' feast in Elsinore. We'll make lots of money there. *Yawns.* Now, I'll sing a little song to myself:

> I am a little bird
> Who sings whate'er he will,
> And when I am in danger
> I fling out a pissing trill
> As in the carnal thrill.

SKAT *speaks*: It's boring to be alone in the forest tonight.

SKAT *sings*: The terrible night doesn't frighten me . . .

He interrupts himself and listens. The sound of industrious sawing is heard through the silence.

SKAT: Workmen in the forest. Oh, well! *Sings.* The terrible night doesn't frighten me . . . Hey, what the devil . . . it's *my* tree they're cutting down.

He peers through the foliage. Below him stands a dark figure diligently sawing away at the base of the tree. SKAT *becomes frightened and angry.*

SKAT: Hey, you! Do you hear me, you tricky bastard? What are you doing with my tree?

The sawing continues without a pause. SKAT *becomes more frightened.*

SKAT: Can't you at least answer me? Politeness costs so little. Who are you?

DEATH *straightens his back and squints up at him.* SKAT *cries out in terror.*

DEATH: I'm sawing down your tree because your time is up.

SKAT: It won't do. I haven't got time.

DEATH: So you haven't got time.
SKAT: No, I have my performance.
DEATH: Then it's cancelled because of death.
SKAT: My contract.
DEATH: Your contract is terminated.
SKAT: My children, my family.
DEATH: Shame on you, Skat!
SKAT: Yes, I'm ashamed.

DEATH begins to saw again. The tree creaks.

SKAT: Isn't there any way to get off? Aren't there any special rules for actors?
DEATH: No, not in this case.
SKAT: No loopholes, no exceptions?

DEATH saws.

SKAT: Perhaps you'll take a bribe.

DEATH saws.

SKAT: Help!

DEATH saws.

SKAT: Help! Help!

The tree falls. The forest becomes silent again.

Night and then dawn.
The travellers have come to a sort of clearing and have collapsed on the moss. They lie quietly and listen to their own breathing, their heartbeats, and the wind in the tree tops. Here the forest is wild and impenetrable. Huge boulders stick up out of the ground like the heads of black giants. A fallen tree lies like a mighty barrier between light and shadow.
MIA, JOF and their child have sat down apart from the others. They look at the light of the moon, which is no longer full and dead but mysterious and unstable.
The KNIGHT sits bent over his chess game. LISA cries quietly behind PLOG's back. JONS lies on the ground and looks up at the heavens.

JONS: Soon dawn will come, but the heat continues to hang

over us like a smothering blanket.
LISA: I'm so frightened.
PLOG: We feel that something is going to happen to us, but we don't know what.
JONS: Maybe it's the day of judgment.
PLOG: The day of judgment ...
> Now something moves behind the fallen tree. There is a rustling sound and a moaning cry that seems to come from a wounded animal. Everyone listens intently, all faces turned towards the sound.
> A voice comes out of the darkness.

RAVAL: Do you have some water?
> RAVAL'S *perspiring face soon becomes visible. He disappears in the darkness, but his voice is heard again.*

RAVAL: Can't you give me a little water? *Pause.* I have the plague.
JONS: Don't come here. If you do I'll slit your throat. Keep to the other side of the tree.
RAVAL: I'm afraid of death.
> *No one answers. There is complete silence.* RAVAL *gasps heavily for air. The dry leaves rustle with his movements.*

RAVAL: I don't want to die! I don't want to!
> *No one answers.* RAVAL'S *face appears suddenly at the base of the tree. His eyes bulge wildly and his mouth is ringed with foam.*

RAVAL: Can't you have pity on me? Help me! At least talk to me.
> *No one answers. The trees sigh.* RAVAL *begins to cry.*

RAVAL: I am going to die. I. I. *I!* What will happen to me! Can no one console me? Haven't you any compassion? Can't you see that I ...
> *His words are choked off by a gurgling sound. He disappears in the darkness behind the fallen tree. It becomes quiet for a few moments.*

RAVAL *whispers*: Can't anyone ... only a little water.
> *Suddenly the* GIRL *gets up with a quick movement,*

> snatches JONS'S *water bag and runs a few steps.* JONS *grabs her and holds her fast.*

JONS: It's no use. It's no use. I know that it's no use. It's meaningless. It's totally meaningless. I tell you that it's meaningless. Can't you hear that I'm consoling you?

RAVAL: Help me, help me!

> *No one answers, no one moves.* RAVAL'S *sobs are dry and convulsive, like a frightened child's. His sudden scream is cut off in the middle.*
> *Then it becomes quiet.*
> *The* GIRL *sinks down and hides her face in her hands.* JONS *places his hand on her shoulder.*

> *The* KNIGHT *is no longer alone.* DEATH *has come to him and he raises his hand.*

DEATH: Shall we play our game to the end?

KNIGHT: Your move!

> DEATH *raises his hand and strikes the* KNIGHT'S *queen. Antonius Block looks at* DEATH.

DEATH: Now I take your queen.

KNIGHT: I didn't notice that.

> *The* KNIGHT *leans over the game. The moonlight moves over the chess pieces, which seem to have a life of their own.*
> JOF *has dozed off for a few moments, but suddenly he wakens. Then he sees the* KNIGHT *and* DEATH *together. He becomes very frightened and awakens* MIA.

JOF: Mia!

MIA: Yes, what is it?

JOF: I see something terrible. Something I almost can't talk about.

MIA: What do you see?

JOF: The knight is sitting over there playing chess.

MIA: Yes, I can see that too and I don't think it's so terrible.

JOF: But do you see who he's playing with?

MIA: He is alone. You *mustn't* frighten me this way.

Jof : No, no, he isn't alone.
Mia : Who is it, then?
Jof : Death. He is sitting there playing chess with Death himself.
Mia : You mustn't say that.
Jof : We must try to escape.
Mia : One can't do that.
Jof : We must try. They are so occupied with their game that if we move very quietly, they won't notice us.

> Jof *gets up carefully and disappears into the darkness behind the trees.* Mia *remains standing, as if paralyzed by fear. She stares fixedly at the* Knight *and the chess game. She holds her son in her arms.*
> *Now* Jof *returns.*

Jof : I have harnessed the horse. The wagon is standing near the big tree. You go first and I'll follow you with the packs. See that Mikael doesn't wake up.

> Mia *does what* Jof *has told her. At the same moment, the* Knight *looks up from his game.*

Death : It is your move, Antonius Block.

> *The* Knight *remains silent. He sees* Mia *go through the moonlight towards the wagon.* Jof *bends down to pick up the pack and follows at a distance.*

Death : Have you lost interest in our game?

> *The* Knight's *eyes become alarmed.* Death *looks at him intently.*

Knight : Lost interest? On the contrary.
Death : You seem anxious. Are you hiding anything?
Knight : Nothing escapes you—or does it?
Death : Nothing escapes me. No one escapes from me.
Knight : It's true that I'm worried.

> *He pretends to be clumsy and knocks the chess pieces over with the hem of his coat. He looks up at* Death.

Knight : I've forgotten how the pieces stood.
Death *laughs contentedly* : But I have not forgotten. You can't get away that easily.

DEATH *leans over the board and rearranges the pieces. The* KNIGHT *looks past him towards the road.* MIA *has just climbed up on the wagon.* JOF *takes the horse by the bridle and leads it down the road.* DEATH *notices nothing; he is completely occupied with reconstructing the game.*

DEATH : Now I see something interesting.
KNIGHT : What do you see?
DEATH : You are mated on the next move, Antonius Block.
KNIGHT : That's true.
DEATH : Did you enjoy your reprieve?
KNIGHT : Yes, I did.
DEATH : I'm happy to hear that. Now I'll be leaving you. When we meet again, you and your companions' time will be up.
KNIGHT : And you will divulge your secrets.
DEATH : I have no secrets.
KNIGHT : So you know nothing.
DEATH : I have nothing to tell.

The KNIGHT *wants to answer, but* DEATH *is already gone.*

A murmur is heard in the tree tops. Dawn comes, a flickering light without life, making the forest seem threatening and evil. JOF *drives over the twisting road.* MIA *sits beside him.*

MIA : What a strange light.
JOF : I guess it's the thunderstorm which comes with dawn.
MIA : No, it's something else. Something terrible. Do you hear the roar in the forest?
JOF : It's probably rain.
MIA : No, it isn't rain. He has seen us and he's following us. He has overtaken us; he's coming towards us.
JOF : Not yet, Mia. In any case, not yet.
MIA : I'm so afraid. I'm so afraid.

The wagon rattles over roots and stones; it sways and creaks. Now the horse stops with his ears flat against

his head. *The forest sighs and stirs ponderously.*
JOF: Get into the wagon, Mia. Crawl in quickly. We'll lie down, Mia, with Mikael between us.
>*They crawl into the wagon and crouch around the sleeping child.*

JOF: It is the Angel of Death that's passing over us, Mia. It's the Angel of Death. *The Angel of Death, and he's very big.*
MIA: Do you feel how cold it is? I'm freezing. I'm terribly cold.
>*She shivers as if she had a fever. They pull the blankets over them and lie closely together. The wagon canvas flutters and beats in the wind. The roar outside is like a giant bellowing.*

>*The castle is silhouetted like a black boulder against the heavy dawn. Now the storm moves there, throwing itself powerfully against walls and abutments. The sky darkens; it is almost like night.*
>*Antonius Block has brought his companions with him to the castle. But it seems deserted. They walk from room to room. There is only emptiness and quiet echoes. Outside, the rain is heard roaring noisily.*
>*Suddenly the* KNIGHT *stands face to face with his wife. They look at each other quietly.*

KARIN: I heard from people who came from the crusade that you were on your way home. I've been waiting for you here. All the others have fled from the plague.
>*The* KNIGHT *is silent. He looks at her.*

KARIN: Don't you recognize me any more?
>*The* KNIGHT *nods, silent.*

KARIN: You also have changed.
>*She walks closer and looks searchingly into his face. The smile lingers in her eyes and she touches his hand lightly.*

KARIN: Now I can see that it's you. Somewhere in your eyes,

somewhere in your face, but hidden and frightened, is that boy who went away so many years ago.

KNIGHT: It's over now and I'm a little tired.

KARIN: I see that you're tired.

KNIGHT: Over there stand my friends.

KARIN: Ask them in. They will break the fast with us.

They all sit down at the table in the room, which is lit by torches on the walls. Silently they eat the hard bread and the salt-darkened meat. KARIN *sits at the head of the table and reads aloud from a thick book.*

KARIN: 'And when the Lamb broke the seventh seal, there was silence in heaven for about the space of half an hour. And I saw the seven angels which stood before God; and to them were given seven trumpets. And another . . .'

Three mighty knocks sound on the large portal. KARIN *interrupts her reading and looks up from the book.* JONS *rises quickly and goes to open the door.*

KARIN: 'The first angel sounded, and there followed hail and fire mingled with blood, and they were cast upon the earth; and the third part of the trees was burnt up and all the green grass was burnt up.'

Now the rain becomes quiet. There is suddenly an immense, frightening silence in the large, murky room where the burning torches throw uneasy shadows over the ceiling and the walls. Everyone listens tensely to the stillness.

KARIN: 'And the second angel sounded, and as it were a great mountain burning with fire was cast into the sea; and a third part of the sea became blood . . .'

Steps are heard on the stairs. JONS *returns and sits down silently at his place but does not continue to eat.*

KNIGHT: Was someone there?

JONS: No, my lord. I saw no one.

KARIN *lifts her head for a moment but once again leans over the large book.*

KARIN: 'And the third angel sounded, and there fell a great

star from heaven, burning as it were a torch, and it fell upon the third part of the rivers and upon the fountains of waters; and the name of the star is called Wormwood . . .'

They all lift their heads, and when they see who is coming towards them through the twilight of the large room, they rise from the table and stand close together.

KNIGHT: Good morning, noble lord.

KARIN: I am Karin, the knight's wife, and welcome you courteously to my house.

PLOG: I am a smith by profession and rather good at my trade, if I say so myself. My wife Lisa — curtsy for the great lord, Lisa. She's a little difficult to handle once in a while and we had a little spat, so to say, but no worse than most people.

The KNIGHT *hides his face in his hands.*

KNIGHT: From our darkness, we call out to Thee, Lord. Have mercy on us because we are small and frightened and ignorant.

JONS *bitterly*: In the darkness where You are supposed to be, where all of us probably are. . . . In the darkness You will find no one to listen to Your cries or be touched by Your sufferings. Wash Your tears and mirror Yourself in Your indifference.

KNIGHT: God, You who are somewhere, who *must* be somewhere, have mercy upon us.

JONS: I could have given you an herb to purge you of your worries about eternity. Now it seems to be too late. But in any case, feel the immense triumph of this last minute when you can still roll your eyes and move your toes.

KARIN: Quiet, quiet.

JONS: I shall be silent, but under protest.

GIRL *on her knees*: It is the end.

JOF and MIA lie close together and listen to the rain tapping lightly on the wagon canvas, a sound which diminishes until finally there are only single drops.

They crawl out of their hiding place. The wagon stands

on a height above a slope, protected by an enormous tree. They look across ridges, forests, the wide plains, and the sea, which glistens in the sunlight breaking through the clouds.

JOF *stretches his arms and legs.* MIA *dries the wagon seat and sits down next to her husband.* MIKAEL *crawls between* JOF'S *knees.*

A lone bird tests its voice after the storm. The trees and bushes drip. From the sea comes a strong and fragrant wind.

JOF *points to the dark, retreating sky where summer lightning glitters like silver needles over the horizon.*

JOF: I see them, Mia! I see them! Over there against the dark, stormy sky. They are all there. The smith and Lisa and the knight and Raval and Jöns and Skat. And Death, the severe master, invites them to dance. He tells them to hold each other's hands and then they must tread the dance in a long row. And first goes the master with his scythe and hourglass, but Skat dangles at the end with his lyre. They dance away from the dawn and it's a solemn dance towards the dark lands, while the rain washes their faces and cleans the salt of the tears from their cheeks.

He is silent. He lowers his hand.

His son, MIKAEL, *has listened to his words. Now he crawls up to* MIA *and sits down in her lap.*

MIA *smiling*: You with your visions and dreams.

*Stockholm
June 5, 1956*